What Makes You Tick

An easy to use guide for understanding basic personality traits, identifying strengths, struggles, and emotional needs.

Open the potential!

Adult Personality Assessment Profile

Kathryn Robbins and Cassandra Cooper

To our families and friends,
who have given us the opportunity to practice what we preach.
We love you.

What Makes You Tick
An easy to use guide for understanding basic personality traits,
identifying strengths, struggles and emotional needs.

The Personality Principles™ assessment profile is a tool in which to help identify a primary personality trait as an aid in personal growth and maturity, not as a test or diagnostic instrument to determine intellectual capacity, metal ability, or mental illness.

info@personalityprinciples.com
PersonalityPrinciples.com

Visit the website to access the online version of this profile
along with more personality information and products.

Archer's Press
St. Louis, MO
ArchersPress.com

Table of Contents

■ ■

Beginning Your Journey

Congratulations! By completing this personality assessment profile you will be taking your first steps toward understanding *what makes you tick*. The reason for completing a personality profile is not to pigeonhole you or limit your options, but to give you a ***You Are Here*** point of reference to start your journey of self-awareness. In learning about your personality type, you will be able to identify your strengths - the things you are naturally good at doing, and your struggles - the behaviors that trip you up in your personal growth and relationships. But, the real benefit of this system is the ability to identify and understand how emotional needs and desires influence behavior patterns - the powerful *why* behind your actions, reactions and behaviors. When you understand the deeper forces that motivate your actions, you can change or modify the behaviors that are causing problems without erasing who you are or having to remake yourself into someone you are not. It's like having your own personalized map to maturity.

There is no right or wrong personality, just different personality traits. The goal in this journey is to move toward maturity, learning to live in your own set of personality strengths and minimize your personality struggles. In order to do this, you need to be able to identify personality traits and behaviors, good and bad, because if nothing changes – nothing changes.

Another beneficial reason for studying personality traits is to take the personal offense out of other people's behavior. If you know the *why* behind their actions, you will understand it has little or nothing to do with you. It's easier to adjust your expectations when you understand their personality type and behavior.

If you can see it – you can adjust it!

After completing the personality assessment, you may find you have a score in each category or there may be one category without a score. This is common. One personality type should stand out more than the others – indicating that this is most likely your primary personality type. Not everyone will have all the traits listed in any one personality type; most people are a blend. By reading about all the personality types, you may get a better insight into your individual blend. To make the system easier to remember, the personality categories have been color coded, eight in all, four primary personality types and four blended personality types. An adjective has also been given to each category as well as the original Greek terms – Sanguine, Choleric, Melancholic and Phlegmatic.

Most people find their personality type first and quickly see the personality types of their family members, friends and co-workers. It's perfectly fine to share your insights with them, but no one likes to be teased or harassed with this information, so please be considerate when sharing. If you have any questions, please feel free to visit the website personalityprinciples.com or email your questions to personalityinfo@gmail.com.

Which personality type is best? The one who is living in their strengths.

"One of a Kind" Character

No matter how many people inhabit the face of the earth, there will never be two people just alike, not even if they are identical twins. The study of human behavior is no simple task – the variables are endless, but that doesn't mean there aren't commonalities that motivate behavior and attitudes. Although there are commonalities, each person's journey is different, which makes a one-of-a-kind character that is all your own.

As we examine **what makes you tick**, we see there are six basic components that go into making up our *character*. Think of mixing these components as if you were mixing colors. Each component adds a new dimension to the mix. (Feel free to read about each personality type before completing the assessment.)

- **Personality** – Recent research suggests that our personality tendencies are heavily influenced by our DNA; you are hardwired with certain personality traits. In order to change your personality completely, you would have to change your DNA. For the purpose of distinguishing personality categories a _color family or hue_ has been assigned to each primary and blend personality types in accordance to the nature of the color itself:
  Primary personality types; **Red**, Yellow, **Blue**, **Green**.
  Blends; Orange (Red & Yellow), **Purple** (Red & Blue), **Teal** (Blue & Green), Yellow Green (Green & Yellow).
  The Personality types will be referred to by these colors.

- **Birth Order** – Studies have shown that our position in our family plays a huge part in imprinting behavior attitudes. Birth order determines the _intensity_ of our personality. Firstborns tend to be more Red, while Lastborns display more Green tendencies. Onlys exhibit the focus of the Blue. Middle Children experience less pressure to be either the leader or the baby, which makes them freer to be more Yellow in their approach to life.

- **Sex or Gender roles** – No doubt about it, men and women are different - hormones reign supreme! Research has shown that testosterone increases aggressiveness, while estrogen increases emotional responses. Society also plays a role in gender behaviors and expectations for men and women.

- **Childhood Experiences** – In childhood we start building the mental and emotional foundations that will be our belief system (self worth) for adult life. Here's where we decide our _value_; are we loved or loathed, smart or stupid, worthy or worthless? This belief system is powerful, but thankfully can be modified throughout our lifetime.

- **Adult Experiences** – Adulthood offers a wide variety of choices higher education, marriage, parenthood, travel, and the freedom to follow our dreams. Adulthood also brings with it responsibility which shapes our choices. These experiences form our habits, attitudes, actions and reactions, which in turn affect our _transparency_, the degree to which we reveal ourselves to others. We can become less or more transparent due to past incidents. Success and pain are experiences that change our perspective, thus changing our attitudes and behaviors.

- **Moral Code** - Culture and religion _tint_ our sense of right and wrong. Your moral code is the foundation on which all other categories rest. This core set of beliefs will be the driving force behind our actions and responses (shame, anger, complacency, repentance, revenge, etc.) when our moral code is challenged or violated.

All these elements mixed together create your *character.*

Begin Your Assessment Here

Instructions:

Read the four statements in each section carefully. Circle the statement that is **MOST like you** when you are feeling relaxed. Try not to over think your answers, just pick what comes naturally to you. There is no right or wrong answer, so be as honest as possible. Most people will have a set of different behaviors at work and home, so try to answer all the questions from one point of view, either at home or at work. You may want to do the profile over from both viewpoints. Your "at home" score will be a truer representation of your personality type.

You should have one statement circled in each section, for a total of 25 selections by the end of the assessment. If there are two answers that are "most" like you, you may choose two, but it is recommended to only pick one answer the first time you do the assessment.

If you feel the results do not match your personality type, do the assessment over, but this time have a friend or family member take the assessment for or with you. If neither of these approaches helped you identify your personality type, redo the assessment, but this time select answers that are **LEAST like you**, eliminating a category each time you redo the assessment, until you are left with only one category.

A	I like to:
1	Talk and tell stories while I work, it helps the time go by faster.
2	Be in charge of the projects, that way I know they will get done.
3	Work on projects by myself, that way I know they are done correctly.
4	Have specific tasks in the project, that way I know what is required of me.
B	**I often feel the need to:**
5	Say my opinion even if it makes others uncomfortable.
6	Redo my work so that it is the best it can be.
7	Agree with other people's opinions in order to keep the situation peaceful.
8	Lighten the mood by making people laugh.
C	**People who know me say:**
9	I am very analytical, and love to research the details.
10	I am a good listener and don't demand my own way.
11	I have never met a stranger – I feel free to talk to anyone about anything.
12	I have never met a challenge I wasn't willing to tackle.
D	**It's difficult for me to:**
13	Assert myself in the presence of powerful people.
14	Stay focused and on task.
15	Not become openly agitated with people who I feel are incompetent.
16	Share personal feelings and desires, unless they are my close companions.

"Personality is only ripe when a man has made the truth his own."

Søren Kierkegaard

E	I like:
17	Attention, even from people who do not know me.
18	To be the leader, because I'm not afraid to make the hard decisions.
19	Privacy, I don't like people probing into my business.
20	Stability, it makes me anxious when things keep changing .

F	When my food order at a restaurant isn't right, I:
21	Point out the mistake and start thinking about reducing the tip. Filling out a comment card with my good or bad opinion, is satisfying to me.
22	Only mention the problem when the server asks if everything is okay. If the server doesn't ask, I would suffer through the meal, but I would consider never eating at that restaurant again.
23	Would pick at the food and find something to eat when I get home.
24	Would question the friends with me, "Did I really order this?"

G	A recurring fear of mine is:
25	Being criticized – what will the neighbors think.
26	Sudden change – loss of security.
27	Loss of social approval – being rejected by people.
28	Being taken advantage of or used for someone else's gain.

H	My number one strength is:
29	Being a team player.
30	Being optimistic.
31	Being resourceful - thinking outside the box.
32	Understanding why details are important.

I	When I'm feeling unusually ill:
33	Call all my friends and warn them that I may have passed on a germ.
34	I keep going – only wimps get sick.
35	I feel concerned and monitor the symptoms to see if they go away.
36	Call my doctor's office and see if I should schedule an appointment.

J	Generally speaking:
37	When I think things are stupid or wrong, I overstep the powers in charge and fix the issues.
38	When my friends and family hurt my feelings, I distance myself and don't talk to them.
39	If I don't like doing a task, I know if I wait long enough, someone else will do it for me.
40	I lose track of my things, like shoes, keys and time.

"At the heart of personality is the need to feel a sense of being lovable without having to qualify for that acceptance."

Paul Tournier

K	It's important to me that people:
41	Understand my deep need for the way I express myself.
42	Appreciate my ability to get along with others.
43	Like me.
44	Support my plan.

L	I feel comforted when:
45	I can relax in my favorite chair.
46	Someone gives me a hug.
47	I've done more than what is on my daily "To Do" list.
48	I have plenty of private time.

M	Much of my success has been from my ability to:
49	Talk my way in and out of anything.
50	Understand failure is just one step closer to success.
51	See the details and understand the difference between good and best.
52	Listen without passing verbal or silent judgment.

N	I prefer my clothing to be:
53	Functional and be "on sale."
54	Well made, classic styling, preferably solid colors.
55	Above all, comfortable - tee shirts rule.
56	Fun, trendy, full of color and movement.

O	Sometimes I come across as:
57	Critical and hard to please.
58	Being too laid back.
59	Being too undisciplined and forgetful of the facts.
60	Too bossy and over bearing, even with strangers.

P	I tend to focus too much on:
61	Keeping the peace.
62	Making everything fun.
63	Being in charge or having a say in how things are run.
64	What others may think.

"If you have anything really valuable to contribute to the world it will come through the expression of your own personality, that single spark of divinity that sets you off and makes you different from every other living creature."

Bruce Barton

Q	I long for:
65	Fun and having a good time.
66	Recognition of my hard work.
67	Solitude and time to think.
68	Someone to notice my good ideas.

R	I can be my best when:
69	Given the freedom to make decisions and explore new ways to streamline the work.
70	There is a systematic approach to the work and enough time to complete the work correctly.
71	There is sense of harmony in the work place with a consistent and steady task schedule.
72	I can openly share my thoughts and be able to physically move around.

S	When I talk:
73	I like to think out what I'm going to say ahead of time. I don't want to be embarrassed.
74	It's usually after everyone else has had a say, I would rather listen more than talk.
75	I talk with my hands – well really with my whole body.
76	People know I'm in charge.

T	I tend to lose:
77	My momentum when overwhelmed with too many details.
78	Track of time when shopping or having fun.
79	Patience with others when they don't get their jobs done.
80	My ability to recover quickly from a disappointment or failure. The pain can be alarming.

U	If given a choice I would:
81	Plan a party and invite tons of friends.
82	Continue working on my projects – I feel I must make hay while the sun shines!
83	Spend time perfecting my creative passion for: music, art, cooking, writing, etc.
84	Rest, maybe even take a nap.

V	I've been appreciated for my ability to:
85	Tackle the hard jobs.
86	Stay on task and focus on each step of the process.
87	Be flexible and accommodating without getting upset.
88	Inspire others with my enthusiasm.

"Too many people overvalue what they are not and undervalue what they are."
Malcolm Forbes

"It is never too late to be who you might have been."
George Eliot

W	Decisions are:
89	Something that should be handled carefully and with research.
90	Hard to make. I would rather let someone else decide for me.
91	Easy for me to make, because I can always change my mind.
92	The thing I do best, because I'm usually right.

X	People say :
93	I am too laid back – I don't feel the need to change the world.
94	I have no concept of time – I tend to be a little on the late side.
95	I am tenacious, I will find a way!
96	I need to lighten-up – I tend to be a bit on the serious side.

Y	One of my pet peeves is when:
97	There isn't any flexibility in the schedule.
98	Incompetent people are in charge.
99	People ignore proper etiquette or protocol.
100	People accuse me of being lazy.

The Personality Principles™ assessment profile is a tool in which to help identify a primary personality trait as an aid in personal growth and maturity, not as a test or diagnostic instrument to determine intellectual capacity, metal ability, or mental illness.

Now that you have made your choices, transfer them to the self-scoring key. Circle the same number in the boxes on the key that you circled in the assessment.

Example: If you have chosen answer 1 in section A, you will circle the number "1" in section A on the self-scoring key, which happens to be in the Playful – Yellow category. Continue transferring your choices for each section. You should have at least 25 choices circled when finished. Now, count up your choices in each column.

The highest score is most likely your primary personality type, while the second highest score will help determine your personality blend.

- There are only four primary personality categories listed on the self-scoring key. These four categories will determine your Primary personality type or personality's base color.
- Most people are a blend of two personality types, having two scores very close to the same.
- Many people have a score, large or small in all four primary categories, however it is not uncommon to have a category with a score of zero (0). This is perfectly fine.
- Some people will have one category with a high score and two others that are close to equal, this is fine also.
- If you feel the category with the highest score does not fit your personality, do the assessment over, or have someone who knows you well do the assessment with you.

Each choice is worth one (1) point. You should not have a score higher than 25 in any one category.

Note: If your two highest scores fall into the Playful Yellow/Proper Blue or Peaceful Green/Powerful Red combinations, please turn to pages 30 and 31 for more information that will help explain your scores.

Self-Scoring Key

Each answer is worth 1 (one) point. Count your choices.

	Playful Sanguine	Powerful Choleric	Proper Melancholic	Peaceful Phlegmatic
A	1	2	3	4
B	8	5	6	7
C	11	12	9	10
D	14	15	16	13
E	17	18	19	20
F	24	21	22	23
G	27	28	25	26
H	30	31	32	29
I	33	34	35	36
J	40	37	38	39
K	43	44	41	42
L	46	47	48	45
M	49	50	51	52
N	56	53	54	55
O	59	60	57	58
P	62	63	64	61
Q	65	66	67	68
R	72	69	70	71
S	75	76	73	74
T	78	79	80	77
U	81	82	83	84
V	88	85	86	87
W	91	92	89	90
X	94	95	96	93
Y	97	98	99	100

Each answer is worth 1 (one) point. Count your choices.

Don not add up your scores like a math equation.

If you scored over 17 points in any category, this is your primary personality – see pages 14, 18, 22, 26.

If you have two scores over 10 points each – you are a blend personality – see pages 16, 20, 24, 28.

If your score is close to (12-6-6-1) you are a combination of three – see page 30.

If all four of your scores are fairly even see pages 30 & 31.

The Personality Principles™ assessment profile is a tool in which to help identify a primary personality trait as an aid in personal growth and maturity, not as a test or diagnostic instrument to determine intellectual capacity, metal ability, or mental illness.

Personal Worksheet

Read the information for each personality type found on pages 14 – 29 before completing this page.

My highest primary personality type score is:_____ in category _____

My second highest personality type score is: _____ in category _____

My Personality Blend category is: _____

Birth Order: [ ] 1st Born [ ] 2nd Born [ ] Middle [ ] Last Born

Sex/Gender: [ ] Male [ ] Female

My personality traits are energized by: [   ] Extravert activities [   ] Introvert activities

My personality traits are attracted to: [   ] People [   ] Tasks

My personality's visible clues are: (These can be from either your Primary or secondary personality type.)
_____
_____
_____

Some of my strengths are (These can be from either your Primary or Secondary personality type.)
_____
_____
_____

Some of my struggles are (These can be from either your Primary or Secondary personality type.)
_____
_____
_____

I feel my deepest emotional needs are (These can be from either your Primary or Secondary personality type.)
_____
_____
_____

As a child, I felt and/or experienced these things that supported or affected my natural personality traits:
_____
_____
_____

As an adult, I felt and/or experienced these things that supported or affected my natural personality traits:
_____
_____
_____

What Makes Me Tick

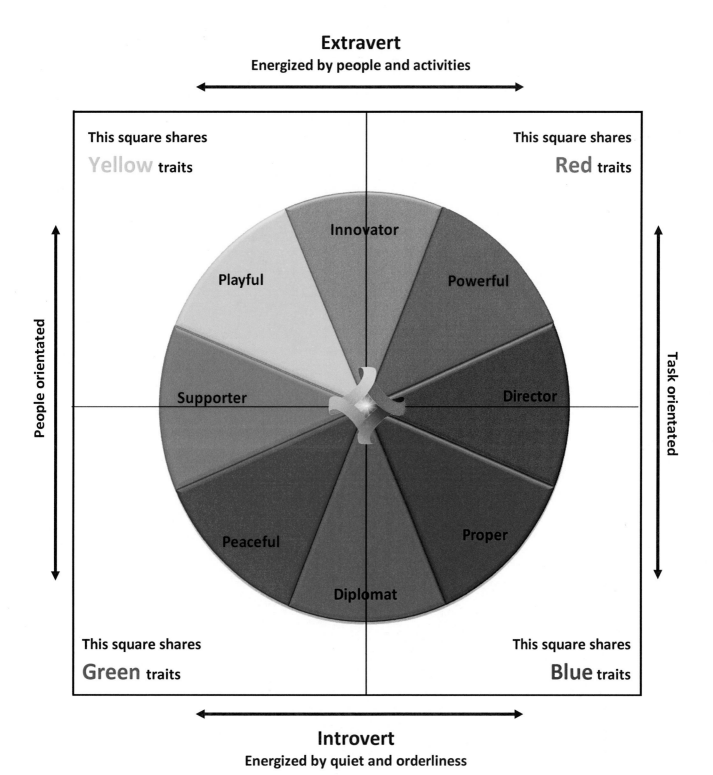

Extravert
Energized by people and activities

This square shares
Yellow traits

This square shares
Red traits

People orientated

Task orientated

Innovator

Playful

Powerful

Supporter

Director

Peaceful

Proper

Diplomat

This square shares
Green traits

This square shares
Blue traits

Introvert
Energized by quiet and orderliness

Playful - Yellow

Playful is a Primary Personality Type
Greek term Sanguine

Visible Clues: Extraverted – People Oriented

Talkative – uses hands while talking
Loves to make people laugh
Attracted to colorful clothing
Loud voice
Open life – tells all
Curious

Optimistic
Dramatic – drama, drama, drama!
Touchy-Feely
Good memory for colors
Makes friends easily
Energetic

Strengths:

Enthusiastic Optimism
Expressive storyteller
Doesn't hold a grudge
Good at motivating people
Volunteers for jobs
Charming salesman
Thrives on activities
 Free Spirited
Affectionate
Spontaneous
Loves people

Struggles:

Interrupts when others are talking
Talks too much – too much information
Naive and gullible
Lacks follow through
Can't say "No"
Exaggerates the truth
Gets bored easily
Dislikes time schedules and deadlines
Gets caught up in sexual misconduct
Irresponsible with time and money
Scatter brained

Desires:

To be liked by everyone
Fun – having a good time

Emotional Needs:

Attention - from all
Acceptance "As Is"
Approval
Affection = physical touch

Famous People

Dolly Parton

Kevin James

Kellie Pickler

Jessica Simpson

Brett Michaels

Steven Tyler

Resembles another personality type when:

Under too much condemnation a Playful will look more like a Peaceful, becoming quieter and more willing to please. This is foraged out of a desperate need to be liked.

Controls by: Turning on the charm

Chances are, if a Playful can get you to laugh or smile, they can get you to change your mind about something – maybe not be as upset with them or get you to do something you didn't want to do.

Playful - Yellow

Communication Style:

Playfuls are open with personal information (TMI – too much information) and use expressive body language. Their hands talk almost as much as their mouth. Laughter comes easily. They are willing to talk to anyone, about anything, at anytime. Their voice carries louder than average, even when talking softly. They are dramatic storytellers, using funny expressions and tends to be a bit long winded. Playfuls touch while talking and have been known to physically hold on to people until the end of their story. They can get lost in conversation by going down rabbit trails, but they don't mind, because life is about the journey not the destination.

Friendship Style:

- **Many best friends** – Playfuls don't limit themselves to just one best friend, there is always room for more friends of equal importance. Sometimes it's hard for their friends to understand this, "I thought I was your best friend!"
- **Warm and inviting** – There is an ease or charm to the way Playfuls share stories, dreams, plans and intimate information, which draws people into the relationship.

Leadership Style:

Playfuls play, so their motive will be centered around everyone having a good time. They volunteer for everything, because it sounds like great fun. They may not know what they are getting into or how to get the job done, but there is always plenty of laughter and lightheartedness and enjoyment.

Excels at:

- **An optimistic attitude** – tomorrow will always be better and they convince others to believe this also.
- **Great memory for color** – many Interior Designers have a bit of Playful in them. They can see very small nuances in color and remember the shade without having the sample with them for comparison.

> **WARNING**
>
> Drama happens!

Blind Spot:

Playfuls fail to see that others take their tardiness, lack of follow-through, and interrupting others during conversations as being disrespectful and rude.

Time management:

- Strengths – Living in the moment, flexibility.
- Struggles – No concept of time, habitually off schedule.

Playfuls embrace what's going on "right now" and have no problem changing their plans, goals, or even their team in order to make it all more enjoyable. They dislike staying on schedule if they're having a good time. They are not wired with an internal clock; five minutes easily turns into forty-five minutes, which is one of the reasons they are habitually late. A lack of being organized is another reason for tardiness.

Goal attitudes:

- Strengths – Optimistic – all things are possible, adaptable.
- Struggles – Pie in the sky dreams, trouble with follow-through.

The Playful's optimistic outlook inspires others to join in on the new "great idea," but they have a difficult time understanding the difference between a measurable goal and an idea full of possibilities. Staying on task can be challenging because they can become easily bored and distracted by bright and shiny objects. They work better as part of a group; they keep the excitement levels up, while the others keep the project on task.

Innovator - Orange

Innovator is a Blend Personality Type
Greek term – Sanguine & Choleric

Visible Clues: Highly Extraverted – People & Task Oriented

Talkative – never met a stranger
Loves to motivate people to action
Clothing is functional and trendy
Commanding tone to voice
Bold and daring
Loves to tells exciting stories

Optimistic
Energetic
Gregarious
Good memory for colors
Likes to have the last word
Willing to put in time to get things done

Strengths:

Charismatic leader
Exudes confidence
Project oriented
Good at motivating people
Energized by a challenge
Persuasive salesman
Thrives on people activities
Clever - resourceful
Usually right
Innovative
Persistent

Struggles:

Charmingly takes over
Overconfident
Workaholic tendency
Bossy
Over-estimates their abilities
Volunteers for too many things
Gets bored easily
Dislikes restrictions
Know-it-all
Self promoting
Talks too much when nervous

Desires:

To be part of the adventure
Closure – getting the loose ends tied

Emotional Needs:

Attention
Credit for their ideas
Accomplishment
Admiration

Resembles another personality types when:

They are happy, they look almost 100% Playful, but when they are upset or under pressure, they can flip the switch and become 100% Powerful.

Controls by: Persuasive salesmanship

Innovators have the energy and determination to wear you down by persistent badgering or pleading their case. They hope you will give in to their requests in order to shut them up.

Famous People

Betty White

Brad Pit

Katy Perry

George Clooney

Paula Dean

Bill Clinton

Innovator - Orange

Communication Style:

An Innovator is a blend of Playful and Powerful, implementing the fun-loving side of the Playful and the big, bold, brave side of the Powerful. With training they can make great public speakers, having no fear of a large audience. They use expressive body movements and facial expressions to emphasize their point. It's not uncommon for Innovators to get off topic or go down rabbit trails, even when on stage.

Friendship Style:

- Networkers – They are the connector people, they know everyone and are very willing to make the necessary introductions, so the needs of the moment are met.
- Dominant – they love being with people, but their subconscious need to be in the lime-light may add stress to some of their relationships.

Leadership Style:

Innovators lead like a Pied Piper. People gravitate towards them because there is fun and laughter going on around them. They are natural born salesman and can get you to "buy in" to almost anything.

Excels at:

- Salesmanship – their optimism can spin any project or plan as being the right one for you!
- Thinking outside the box – because they see rules as "suggestions" they are free to investigate new innovative ways to get the job done.

Blind Spot:

Innovators fail to see their competitive nature, they view it as being enthusiastic, but this unbridled behavior can cause them to overstep their boundaries and get voted off the team.

> **WARNING**
>
> Lead, Follow
> or
> Get out of the way

Time management:

- Strengths – Adaptable, and does well with deadlines.
- Struggles – Overextended; has a hard time saying no, easily distracted.

Innovators use deadlines to help keep them on track, even if they have to burn the midnight oil to get it all done. They have a charitable adaptability – they will set their projects aside to help with your project, even if it means giving up sleep to make sure everything is done on time. Innovators share the Playful's struggle to say NO, for two reasons - they want people to like them and they are good at fixing problems. Between curious quests and problem solving, distractions become a lifestyle.

Goal attitudes:

- Strengths – Confident, innovative.
- Struggles – Time management, chasing bright and shiny objects.

Innovators enjoy coming up with "out of the box" solutions to problems. Even if an attempt fails, they are convinced that it will eventually work if you just hang in there and keep trying. Their willingness to rescue others will cause them to over commit and sometimes derail their personal goals and plans, but this doesn't always bother them as it gives them a sense of accomplishment. They also have a hard time narrowing their interests – they want to do it all!

Powerful - Red

Powerful is a Primary Personality Type
Greek term - Choleric

Visible Clues: Extravert – Task Oriented

Takes charge naturally
Not concerned with what others think
Clothing must be functional – pockets
Has a commanding presence
Competitive
Says what's on their mind

Risk taker
Thinks big
No nonsense approach to life
Finger pointing and fist pounding to make a point
Adventurous – physical activity
Hates to be sick or incapacitated

Strengths:

Determined
Natural born leader - Hard worker
Decisive
Loves to be challenged
Direct
Problem Solver
Good instinct – usually right
Exudes confidence
Outside the box thinker
Takes responsibility
Self starter

Struggles:

Argumentative
Bossy - Task master
Decides for everyone
Reckless
Blunt and tactless
Usurper – takes over
Belligerent - doesn't listen to advice
Arrogant
The end justifies the means
Lets others take the blame
Blindly stubborn

Desires:

To be in charge
Fix things (people, places, ideas) that are broken

Emotional Needs:

Closure
A sense of control
Loyalty
Credit for their hard work

Famous People

Simon Cowell

Mother Teresa

Henry Ford

Kathryn Hepburn

Donald Trump

Margaret Thatcher

Resembles another personality type when:
Life is going smoothly and they are happy – they become chattier and high spirited resembling an Innovator, but at a moment's notice they are still ready and willing to rule the world. (Of all personality types, Powerfuls stay more true to their personality traits.)

Controls by: Fits of anger
When a Powerful doesn't get their way they throw a fit, sometimes it becomes rage. All of this can be very scary and they like it that way, because they know you will rarely challenge them which gives them the control.

Powerful - Red

Communication Style:

The Powerful personality type wants to know the bottom line first, doesn't care much for chit-chat; "Get to the point." Moves on when they have grasped the concept. Their talk is full of intensity, giving quick commands or orders. For emphasis, they use fist pounding and pull out a "bony finger in your face." They like to complain about things they feel are stupid, even if they plan to follow through with it anyway. They have little tolerance for incompetence. No need to wonder if they are mad at you – without a doubt you'll know.

Friendship Style:

- Intense – Powerfuls say what's on their mind and often tell friends what they should or shouldn't be doing.
- Productive – they invest in others when there is potential, but don't spend much time developing relationships they feel are a waste of time. They either find others of like kind who are industrious, or they become loners.

Leadership Style:

Powerfuls are natural born leaders, either leaders of the good guys or the bad guys, but no matter what, they naturally take the lead. They always have a plan and a purpose. People are attracted to their bold and fearless approach to life. For the most part Powerfuls are honest and people can trust them with their lives.

Excel at:

- Getting the job done – closure energizes them, so the more that can be checked off the list the better they feel and the more they feel like doing.
- Seeing the bigger picture – Powerfuls see more than the project, they envision the future.

Blind Spot:

Powerfuls feel they have the right to speak their mind whenever they wish, believing this to be an honest approach to life, but when others do that to them, they get their feelings hurt, which is expressed in angry outbursts. They would do better to understand what hurts the goose hurts the gander.

Time management:

- Strengths – Multitasking, and determined goal setter.
- Struggles – Impatient, can't turn off their brain – has a hard time resting (struggles with insomnia).

Powerfuls think the world would be a better place if they were the gatekeepers of time; they hate wasted time and effort. Multitasking is their way of getting the most done in the least amount of time. Being kept waiting is a fate worse than death, even if there is no way around it. Powerfuls have a hard time shutting down; their brain keeps on going long after their body has called it a day.

Goal attitudes:

- Strengths – Visionary, can see the bigger picture, competitive, doesn't get sidetracked easily.
- Struggles – Impatient, needs to accomplish, over controlling (usurping).

Powerfuls are compelled to start the project before all the small details are figured out. There's almost nothing more fulfilling than seeing the goal completed and crossed off the list. Powerfuls may not always consider another's feelings, time, or energy in the fulfillment of the goal. When working with a team, they need to understand the other team members also have talents and they should use these strengths wisely to reach the goal's conclusions.

Director - Purple

Director is a Blend Personality Type
Greek term – Choleric & Melancholic

Visible Clues: Extravert & Introvert – Task Oriented

You can feel the intensity if their personality
Well put together – expensive clothing
More serious than lighthearted
Exacting – knows what they want
Good time manager
Good with numbers

Articulate
Hard worker
Extremely organized
Connoisseur of fine things
Not overly flashy or warm
Impatient - They don't suffer fools well

Strengths:

Organized
Leader of leaders
Trail blazer
Problem solver
Radiates confidence
Methodical – thinks it through
High standards
Systematic
Soft hearted
Hard worker
Connoisseur

Struggles:

Obsessive compulsive
Dictator
Obstinate
Co-dependent rescuer
Egotistical
Hyper critical
Very hard to please
Short tempered
Sharp tongue
Heavy-handed
Unrealistic expectations

Desires:

To be right
Organized, so the job can be completed

Emotional Needs:

A sense of influence
Accomplishment
Consideration of their feelings
Private space

Resembles other personality types when:

Content, they mimic the strengths of the Innovator – talkative, upbeat, charming and full of plans for the future, but when down or depressed, they look like the Diplomat living in their struggles – bullheaded, procrastinates, tells lies and is unwilling to take responsibility for their actions; blaming others for their situation.

Controls by: Holding information hostage

Directors can radiate just as much fear as the Powerfuls, but are a bit more passive-aggressive. Most of the time they choose to quietly withhold important information that you need, making the job harder or you look bad in front of others.

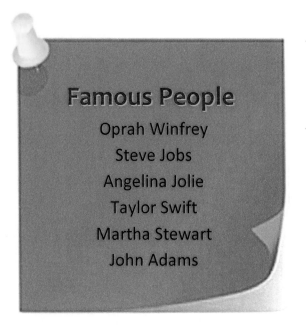

Famous People

Oprah Winfrey

Steve Jobs

Angelina Jolie

Taylor Swift

Martha Stewart

John Adams

Director - Purple

Communication Style:

The Director is a blend of Powerful and Proper. They tend to be forward thinkers who speak their minds without fear. They are focused and accurate, becoming impatient with those who are not. They can hold a secret or thought for a very long period of time, if not forever. For the most part they appear to be cool, calm and in control, but can become unreasonable when overly emotional, triggering wide intense mood swings and behaviors.

Friendship Style:

- Loyal – Directors are more attached to principles, ideas or a cause than to individual people, but when they are attached to a person (or animal), it will be all-out devotion.
- Hot and cold – Their ability or inability to handle their feelings will dictate the health of their relationships. The "it" list and "hit" list are updated on a regular basis. One day you're in, the next day you could be out.

Leadership Style:

The Director, when living in strengths, is probably the most effective leader of all. This happens by combining the ability to analyze data and the drive to move forward. If you like them or not they command respect, because of their results.

Excel at:

- Management – They can see the bigger picture while being able to divide the project into smaller parts.
- Organization – using the ability to analyze and understand why particular things need to be in a certain place or order, helps Directors streamline operations, be it running a business or household.

Blind Spot:

Directors desire the best things in life, and have a sense of entitlement, sometimes making others feel like indentured servants in their pursuit of all life has to offer. They have great memories, but this can lead to lengthy grudge holding.

Time management:

- Strengths – Detailed planners, stay focused and on track
- Struggles – Inconsiderate, self-centered interests.

Time is the most valuable commodity Directors have – each minute is viewed in terms of productivity. Directors are extremely organized, which helps keeps them on task. Even if the schedule bends slightly, any task will be completed on time; this may inconvenience others, but "that's just the price of doing business." Of course, their ideas and goals are the best, no matter what others may think.

Goal attitudes:

- Strengths – Strategists, laser focused
- Struggles – Unsympathetic, Imposes their standards on others

Directors will view their goal with extreme scrutiny in order to refine the best approach, knowing which steps to take and when to make them. Because of the high regard they have for their own ideas and standards, when they have their plans in order they assume others will willingly follow, even if this plan inconveniences those involved. They are not always willing to hear another's point of view without an argument.

Proper - Blue

Proper is a Primary Personality Type
Greek term – Melancholic

Visible Clues: Introvert – Task Oriented

Proper – needs to follow the rules
Strives for perfection
Quiet and reserved
Maintains high standards
Irritated by ignorant people
Second guesses their decisions

Loves to study - Analytical
Private with thoughts and plans
Organizes with charts and graphs
Conservative clothing - Khaki, gray, navy blue etc.
Focuses on precise details
Concerned about health issues and germs

Strengths:

Strives for excellence
Analytical
Likes to have life scheduled
High standards
Works well alone
Good listener
Artistic
Careful
Empathetic
Diligent researcher

Struggles:

Obsessive
Gets lost in the details
Inflexible
Unreasonably picky
Jealous of others
Silently condemning
Eccentrically self indulgent
Overly fearful
Takes everything personally
Self sabotage

Desires:

To have privacy
Propriety – rules are important

Emotional Needs:

Alone time
Silence
Understanding for their preferences
Sensitivity to their feelings

Famous People

Meryl Streep

Johnny Depp

Sarah Brightman

Steve Martin

Mark Zuckerberg

Enya

Resembles another personality type when:

They need to present a certain persona – they can be charming like a Playful in short bursts, like at a dinner party and are able to immerse themselves in any personality type for a role on stage or screen production. Some of the best actors and actresses are Propers.

Controls by: Moodiness or depression

Two forces come into play – Propers want to be left alone and know that people will give others space if they aren't feeling on top of their game. Secondly, if they can get you focused on their problems, they don't have to accommodate yours.

Proper - Blue

Communication Style:

Propers are the most reserved with their spoken words, but many times they are the most prolific communicators in written form; books, poetry, music, art, etc. They tend to be reserved in their body language as well; gestures are careful and close to the body. You can feel the boundaries of their personal space. Their voice tone is soft and metered. The more comfortable they are, the quieter their voice becomes.

Friendship Style:

- Selective – Propers are comfortable being by themselves, so if they are going to share their dreams, goals and passions, it will have to be with the right people or person.
- Few close friends - one good friend is enough. This close friend could be a spouse or family members.

Leadership Style:

Their leadership style is cautious and premeditated. Titles are to be respected and proper decorum followed. They are reluctant leaders, because of self doubt, even though they have the ability to be great leaders.

Excels at:

- Analytical thinking – being able to tell the difference between good and best, gives them the cutting edge in the arts, sciences, and literary pursuits.
- Focused discipline – Propers take the time to research where they want to go and how they want to get there, with the willingness to limit their lives in order to attain that goal.

WARNING

High maintenance required

Blind Spot:

The Proper personality type is private with personal information, feeling more comfortable expressing feelings and thoughts through the arts; music, poetry, drawing, acting, etc.. Propers withhold opinions or information and share only on a "need to know" bases. They will open up only if they feel safe from criticism or ridicule. Because of the Proper's emotional sensitivity, they are prone to take remarks as personal attacks, even if the comments had nothing to do with them. Hold a grudge or plotting revenge, may be their way of responding to such situations, leaving the other person clueless as to why the relationship is now suffering.

Time management:

- Strengths – Focused, and scheduled.
- Struggles – Stingy when giving time to others, secretive about their plans.

Propers usually have a daily planner and religiously live by it. They arrive on time, if not a bit early. They prefer to concentrate on one activity at a time and do not like being rushed. They don't want to make a mistake, so they prefer to work alone so as not to have others mess things up.

Goal attitudes:

- Strengths – Meticulous planner. Disciplined
- Struggles – Fear of all that could go wrong. Over analyzes the details.

Propers are detailed planners, only moving forward after all options are well researched. They execute their goals with personal discipline – a place for everything and everything in its place. They may see challenges as obstacles, and feel overwhelmed by the fear of failure. When this happens they tend to start over-analyzing as a form of procrastination.

Diplomat - Teal

Diplomat is a Blend Personality Type

Greek term – Melancholic & Phlegmatic

Visible Clues: Highly Introverted – People & Task Oriented

Patient Listeners
Well mannered
Low Key
Well liked by the majority
Compassionate and empathetic
Waxes philosophical and poetic

Dry sense of humor
Conservative in clothing
Quiet and reserved
Methodical
Loyal
Enjoys tinkering

Strengths:

Excellent listener
Steady worker
Loyal
Well liked
Considerate
Studious
Diplomatic
Likes charts and graphs
Quiet – low key
Works well alone
Cautious

Struggles:

Silently opinionated
Stunted under pressure
Worrier - fearful
Compromises standards
Takes on other people's pain
Pessimistic
Secretive – sneaky
Hard to get moving
Procrastinates
Intolerant of others
Saboteur – undermines others

Desires:

Time to think things over
People to "know" what they need without having to say it out loud

Emotional Needs:

Private down time
Compassion for their feelings
Lack of interruptions
Rest

Resembles other personality types when:

They feel comfortable and secure, words, thoughts and feelings all bubbling to the surface and pouring out at once, making them look like a Playful, but this is only an occasional occurrence, not an everyday behavior.

Famous People

Jimmy Carter

Garrison Keillor

Sandra Bullock

Charles Darwin

Stephen King

Prince William

Controls by: Sabotage

Diplomats have the patience of the Peaceful and the methodical focus of the Proper, so it's not uncommon for the plan to take days, weeks, months or maybe even years to unfold depending on the desired result – revenge or peacekeeping.

Diplomat - Teal

Communication Style:
The Diplomat is a blend of Proper and Peaceful. They try to live by the saying, "If you can't say anything nice, say nothing at all." They will guide a conversation into neutral territory hoping to keep things calm and friendly. When possible they think out what they plan to say, so as not to be offensive. When they feel secure they become very talkative. The fear of saying something wrong or hurtful is always at the forefront of their minds.

Friendship Style:
- Respectful – Diplomats usually have many friends, because they are respectful of personal boundaries. For the most part they keep their opinions to themselves.
- Cautious – Intimate friendships are reserved for those closest to them: a spouse, sibling(s) or their children. Sharing their deeper feelings and ideas is not offered to the general friendship list.

Leadership Style:
Diplomats approach leadership with a bit of reluctance, but humbly serve the group. They can see both sides of a topic, but are often swayed by a sob story. When living in their strengths, a Diplomat is prepared and orderly, kind and understanding, developing a devout following. Their leadership style is more like a shepherd.

Excels at:
- Research and Development – Diplomats have the focus of the Proper and the steadiness of the Peaceful making them some of the best technicians and information compilers around.
- School or Studies - When they have a project to do, they are steady workers – when they are on, they are on, but when they are off, they are off. Doing quieter things such as studying is enjoyable to them.

WARNING

Fear holding up progress

Blind Spot:
Diplomats are hard to get moving, as the fear of the unknown or the desire to do it perfectly can impede progress. Diplomats are willing to live in undesirable conditions for fear of not being able to correct the situation to proper standards. Nor are they willing to let others do the work for them – delegation is not their strong point.

Time management:
- Strengths – Dependable, and compassionate to others' troubles.
- Struggles – Hard to motivate, stubborn when pushed.

Diplomats will always make time to listen with sincere compassion and they appear to have an unlimited supply of time to deal with others. Overcoming inertia is a trial. Diplomats will dig their heels in if pushed out of their comfort zone. Procrastination is their way of controlling their environment.

Goal attitudes:
- Strengths – Methodical, Cautious
- Struggles – Can't start until all the research is done, apprehensive

They map out a tangible plan, investigating all possible problems and search for solutions to these issues before starting any project. Apprehension to move forward can be an indication of anxiety or avoiding stress which can be conflict or confrontation. Many times "research" becomes the excuse for not moving forward.

Peaceful - Green

Peaceful is a Primary Personality Type
Greek term – Phlegmatic

Visible Clues: Introvert – People Oriented

Easy going
Patient
Has a hard time making decisions
Team Player
Low pain threshold
Comfortable clothing – knit and elastic

Likable
Seeks to be at peace with all
Picky eater
Good Listener
Witty – one liner sense of humor
Hard to motivate

Strengths:

Friendly
Easy going – low key
Cooperative
Even tempered
Loyal
Steady worker
Kind – nice
Good listener
Peacemaker
Reliable
Content

Struggles:

Becomes a chameleon
Lazy
Doormat
Procrastinate
Will of iron when pushed
Workaholic – uses work as a protection
Tells lies or part truths to make others fell good
Uninvolved
Peace at all costs
Hard to get moving
Boring

Desires:

To be at peace - with everyone, everywhere
Comfort – food, clothing, furniture, relationships

Emotional Needs:

Feelings of Worth
Rest = Sleep
Peace – minimal conflict
Comfort

Resembles another personality type when:

In leadership - Peacefuls get promoted due to their ability to be loyal to the plan, making them look more like a Powerful. They can also resemble a Proper in the ability to be single-mindedly focused on a project or hobby to the extraction of all else.

Controls by: Procrastination

Most people procrastinate on things they don't want to do, but the Peacefuls use procrastination on purpose, like a tool. This behavior is linked to two sources; low energy – if I wait long enough someone else will do it and because decision making is very hard for the Peaceful, so if they wait long enough, it will be made for them, either by default or by someone else stepping in and doing it.

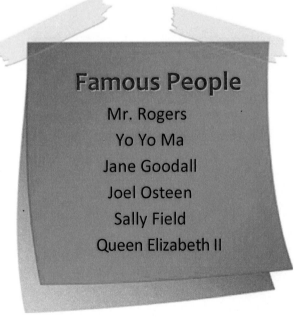

Famous People

Mr. Rogers

Yo Yo Ma

Jane Goodall

Joel Osteen

Sally Field

Queen Elizabeth II

Peaceful - Green

Communication Style:

Peacefuls have a soft voice. They hesitate to jump into conversations, but enjoy listening to others talk. Their desire is a peaceful environment, so they look for kind things to say about others and avoid conflict by telling you what you want to hear. They enjoy a relaxed comfortable conversation one-on-one, but can be easily overpowered when too many people are talking at once.

Friendship Style:

- Faithful – Peacefuls are some of the most loyal friends. They choose to see the good and overlook the faults.
- Kind – Because they feel no need be in competition with others, they are free to give compliments and be nice without expecting repayment as long as it doesn't require too much effort.

Leadership Style:

When placed in leadership, their style is more of a shepherd; personal one-on-one, caring and full of grace, tending to the individual needs of each person in the group.

Excels at:

- Finding the middle ground – because they value peace and do not feel the over whelming need to win or be right, they can see both sides to an issue and help others make the adjustments needed.
- Hard worker – They are the unsung heroes of the work force. There are more quiet workaholics in this personality category than any other.

Blind Spot:

Peacefuls have difficulty making decisions, so when others step in and make the decision for them, they feel bullied or pushed. When this happens over and over, feelings of resentment start to build and passive-aggressive behaviors come into play eroding the stability in their relationships, be it at work or in their home life.

Time management:

- Strengths – Steady, accommodating
- Struggles – Procrastination, and moves slowly

Peacefuls function well in a routine, taking one step in the project at a time. Flying by the seat of their pants is okay, but is too stressful as a way of life. They are not normally upset if their schedules are out of order, so helping someone else is fine with them. Indecision and putting things off come naturally to the Peaceful, so it is not uncommon for a project to take "three years and thirty minutes." Peacefuls have the lowest amount of energy, they move at a slower pace than the rest of the personality types and need more rest than others.

Goal attitudes:

- Strengths – Consistency, works well in a routine
- Struggles – Complacent, lack of foresight

For the Peaceful, most goals will be part of a routine, something to be learned and incorporated into daily life. Peacefuls love stability and once they have committed to a goal, will show great willpower and perseverance to see it accomplished. Peacefuls don't anticipate future problems; they just handle things as they happen. Their goals are frequently directed by an outside influence such as: health issues, money matters, or relationships.

Supporter - Yellow Green

Supporter is a Blend Personality Type

Greek term – Sanguine & Phlegmatic

Visible Clues: Introvert & Extravert – People Oriented

Friendly
Comfortable and fun clothing
Flexible
Hates to be alone
Easily distracted
Self sacrificing

Easy going and enjoyable
Tries to make other people happy
Often arrives late
Usually in a good mood
Easily overwhelmed
Absentminded

Strengths:

Likes people
Forgiving
Optimistic
Easy going - fun loving
Talkative
Willing volunteer
Generous
Kindhearted
Curious
Affectionate
Cheerful

Struggles:

Obnoxious
Forgetful
Naive
Losses track of time
Interrupts others while they are talking
Over extends schedule
Lack of boundaries
Gullible
Easily distracted
Sexual misconduct
Needs to be rescued

Desires:

To be noticed and be part of the action
Things to be trouble-free and easy

Emotional Needs:

Connection – friendship
To be noticed
Stress-free environment
Relaxation

Resembles other personality types when:

For the most part Supporters don't change their behavior, but under stress they can look more like a Diplomat - quiet and lost in the details.

Controls by: The need to be rescued

Although Supporters are quite capable of getting the job done, they underestimate the time needed to do the job or they put too much on the schedule, or oversell their abilities, so their friends and family come to their aid. This meets the need to be noticed and be connected to others.

Famous People

Michelle Duggar

Kurt Russell

Drew Barrymore

Bruce Jenner

Tim Allen

Kate Middleton

Supporter- Yellow Green

Communication Style:

The Supporter is a combination of Playful and Peaceful. Their goal is to have a good time: tell stories, laughing and have everyone get along. They are affectionate and friendly, so they may touch others while talking to them. They can become overly excitable and distracted when there is either too much fun or fear involved in a situation.

Friendship Style:

- Everybody's best friend – They love everyone and for the most part, everyone loves them. They are easy going and always willing to go out and have fun.
- Generous – Supporters are compassionate and have huge generous hearts. If they see others in need, they will gather together the people and supplies to meet that need, be it for the homeless, military families or natural disaster relief efforts. They can be great fund raisers too.

Leadership Style:

Supporters are good team players, willing to take the lead, coming up with great ideas of what can be done, but if they are living in struggles, they may need an accountability partner to make sure the plans are organized and finished. Their deepest desire is to create fun and camaraderie, but can become over committed, because they don't want to miss out on anything. Warm, inviting and kind, they are well liked even when their leadership style is shaky.

Excel at:

- Being a good sounding board – Supporters have the Peaceful's ability to listen without passing judgment, so people like bouncing ideas off of them. They don't feel it's their job to fix others.
- Making others feel welcomed – They share the openness of the Playful, which draws people in, making them feel welcome and secure.

WARNING

Chasing
shiny objects

Blind Spot:

They struggle with making decisions, not out of fear they will make a wrong decision, but because they really don't know what they want. Money slips through their fingers for lack of keeping track of totals. Supporters have a hard time believing that anything bad will happen. Ignorance is bliss.

Time management:

- Strengths – Cooperative, and generous
- Struggles – Indecisive and naive as to time frames

Supporters always have time to add another activity when it comes to helping a friend, even if it cause them to become late and over extended. Because sharing time and possessions comes easily to a Supporter, they struggle with time frames; before they know it, one minute turns into ten minutes; by the end of the day their schedule is way off course.

Goal attitudes:

- Strengths – Pliable, works well toward a common goal
- Struggles – Easily overwhelmed, gives up quickly

Supporters work best in a group, being able to adjust to different ideas and approaches to the project. They can easily support someone else's goals and work toward that end, but without a clear agenda, they can become easily overwhelmed and confused as to what they are supposed to be doing. It helps to have a defined outcome and end date, as this helps to break larger projects into manageable parts.

Combination of Three

Sometimes, when a primary personality trait is very strong (50% or higher) the two personality traits on either side of this category (see chart) will behave equally, giving the impression of a learned personality, however a truly learned personality will not have the stability the strong primary personality trait offers. A learned personality will fluctuate between polar opposites (Playful/Proper or Powerful/Peaceful).

Let's say you scored a 13 in the Powerful (Red) category, a 5 in the Playful (Yellow), 6 in the Proper (Blue) and a 1 in the Peaceful (Green) categories. So what does this mean? Your primary personality type is first and foremost Powerful Choleric, (large and in charge) with wings in both Playful (fun) and Proper (scheduled). A person with a score such as this will exhibit traits of the primary personality most of the time, with undertones of the other two personality types. There is nothing "wrong" with combinations of three as long as the "wings" are on the adjoining sides of the primary personality category.

If your scores indicate a different combination, like – Playful 13, Powerful 5, Proper 6 and Peaceful 1, please read about the Learned Personality on page 31 and take the profile over again. Chances are you over thought your answers or misunderstood the questions. If need be, have someone who knows you well take the profile with you.

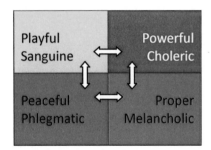

Here are the natural combinations of three:

Playful Sanguine – wings: Powerful Choleric and Peaceful Phlegmatic

Powerful Choleric – wings: Proper Melancholic and Playful Sanguine

Proper Melancholic – wings: Peaceful Phlegmatic and Powerful Choleric

Peaceful Phlegmatic – wings: Playful Sanguine and Proper Melancholic

Combination of Four

On occasion a person's score may come out even across all four personality categories. This may happen for several reasons.

- The person taking the profile has a difficult time acknowledging their true behaviors.
- They may hate the feeling of being "pigeonholed" and decide to choose random answers.
- They may have learned a personality trait and are not aware it's not really who they are.
- They may have a hard time making decisions, especially introspective ones.

Having an even score happens more often to the Peaceful Phlegmatic personality category than any other category. There's several reasons for this. First is, they have a harder time making decisions, not because they fear making the wrong one, they just don't know which is the right one. Second, it takes a lot of emotional energy to think introspectively and the Peaceful personality type has the lowest natural energy levels.

If your scores came out even, read the personality descriptions on pages 14 – 29, and complete the profile again.

The Learned Personality

Learned - Behavior or knowledge that is acquired through training or experience rather than being instinctual.

Coping - Come to terms with, or to shape, or conform to the shape of another member.

Disguising - Hidden under a false appearance.

To love and be loved, is what life is all about, so when love becomes conditional our behavior will modify to the demands of the person we want to be loved by in order to get the "good stuff" in the relationship. This could be parent to child, spouse to spouse, or friend to friend. In some cases this can even be boss to employee.

Personality Principles™ addresses the issues of a learned personality or masking our real self, holding to the belief that the blend of Proper Melancholic--Playful Sanguine or Powerful Choleric--Peaceful Phlegmatic personality blend is not a natural blend, but rather a learned way of living. For instance, if a person who is open, bubbly, chatty, and loves being the center of attention one day, swings the other way, becoming shy, deeply private, shunning attention and very focused about small details the next, you have confusion. This swing in behavior will drain a person's emotional energy, to say nothing of how confusing this will be for the people who are in a relationship with them. Trying to be something you are not is hard work.

Note: These conditions are not the only reasons for a learned personality, nor should you consider your personality learned if you have experienced any of these situations.

Probable Causes

- A domineering parent or one with unrealistic expectations. This type of parent can create an environment where a child learns behaviors or survival skills that are not instinctive to their personality type in order to please the parent and hopefully be loved in return.
- A domineering or overly controlling spouse/partner. This can be a similar situation as with a domineering parent, only these relationships start out voluntary and require other methods of control, such as codependency, temper tantrums, blaming, guilt, verbal abuse or violence.
- Living in a home with substance abuse (alcohol or drugs). Many home environments become more secretive and codependent where substance abuse takes place. Alcoholics Anonymous and Al-Anon can help unlearn some of these behaviors.
- Severe illness or extreme dysfunction (mental illness) may also cause unnatural pressures on a dependent child to perform adult duties or contribute to the household, often assuming a parental role.
- Some forms of emotional or physical abuse may lead to the child conforming to the demands of the abusing parent in hopes of stopping the harsh treatment.
- Childhood sexual interference or violation may cause the child to exaggerate natural behaviors or take on behaviors not natural to his/her personality type, such as attention seeking or lying for no reason.
- Growing up in a single-parent home might result in some form of personality coping, especially if the child is firstborn, in which case the child may fulfill some of the roles of the absent parent.
- Legalistic religious homes or those with intense regulatory standards can stifle a person's natural personality, causing the person to think there is something "wrong" with them, because they aren't like the others.

> "What you see, you learn – What you learn, you practice –
> What you practice, you become – What you become has consequences."
> Earnie Larsen

Understanding Emotional needs

Emotional Needs are not wants; these needs are the source of how we recharge our emotional batteries. They are on the same level of need as air, food, water, shelter -- in this instance, our emotional health. It's what makes us feel loved. There are no right or wrong needs, just different needs for each personality type.

Here's a quick list of the most important emotional needs for each of the personality types. Most people are a combination of two or three personality types, so you may want to write down the needs that resonate most with you even if they are listed in another personality type than your highest score(s).

Playful - Yellow

Attention – from any and all. Playfuls love to be the center of attention. This could be the subliminal reason Playfuls love to wear bright colors and it may even be the reason their voices carry louder than most. They don't even mind being embarrassed or the object of the joke - bad attention is better than no attention.

Acceptance "As Is" - This type of acceptance can resemble mild forgiveness. Playfuls have good self-esteem built-in and are surprised to find that others may not like them, but instead of working to gain acceptance, they use charm to get back into others' good graces. After all, what's not to love?!

Approval – This is one of the main reasons why they can't say "No." They really, really want you to like them. Playfuls will become almost chameleon-like when seeking approval from those who matter most to them. Desperate, destructive, needy behaviors can develop if this need is not met in proactive ways.

Affection = physical touch – Human touch is love to a Playful. To be held and cuddled is what life is all about. If this need is withheld from them for too long, they will find it somewhere with someone. When physical touch goes unmet, the temptation for sexual misconduct is close at hand.

Innovator - Orange

Attention – The Innovator, being part Playful shares the same emotional need of attention, only it becomes much more competitive because there is Powerful - Red in this blend type also. Innovators are natural entertainers, breaking into spontaneous comedy routines, or heading up group activities. They attract attention due to all the noise, activity and energy that surrounds them.

Credit for their ideas – Innovators are out-of-the-box thinkers; resourceful and clever, so when their ideas work they want to see their name in lights, on the cover and/or an award which identifies them as the person who thought up this idea. When feeling needy, they may even steal the credit for someone else's work.

Accomplishment – As a blend of Playful and Powerful, the Innovator has a double portion of extraverted personality traits and the energy to go along with it. They need to see progress and are willing to roll up their sleeves to make it happen. Accomplishment leads to attention, credit, and admiration, which all recharges their batteries.

Admiration – Applause, an At-A-Boy, an award, or a thank you card, are all forms of admiration that work well for the Innovator. A career in sales or the entertainment industry is ideal for the Innovator. If the emotional need of admiration is not met properly, narcissistic behaviors can develop.

Understanding Emotional needs

Powerful - Red

Closure - If at the end of a day, a Powerful hasn't crossed enough items off their to-do list, they will find it hard to turn their brain off or fall asleep. In fact, they have been known to get out of bed in the middle of the night and tackle a small project, just to check it off the list, so their brain will shut down and go to sleep.

A sense of control - Powerfuls love to be in charge. They have built-in ego strength to get the job done, which make them question everything that's going on. "Why are we doing it this way? Wouldn't it work better if we..? I have a plan as to how this can work better!" They always have a plan. Without a plan, they feel like life is in a free-fall. Some of the need for control is fear based, but they may not want to admit that.

Loyalty - They will work long and hard if there is support from the powers-that-be. A Powerful may even be willing to be the spokesman for the group if a problem needs to be addressed, but the group better not leave them hanging when opposition takes place, or there will be some angry out-bursts. If left hanging, the Powerful will never lift a finger to help that team's cause again; they will cut their losses and move on.

Credit for their hard work - Powerfuls go a long way on a small amount of whole-hearted appreciation for their efforts. They do not require tons of mushy-gushy praise, or their name in lights, but if they feel used or taken advantage of, they will stop working hard and let the chips fall where they may.

Director – Purple

A sense of influence – As a blend of Powerful and Proper, the Director has a more tolerant approach when it comes to controlling the world around them. More than having a vote or getting their way all the time, Directors want to set the course and steer the ship, which all takes careful planning and time.

Accomplishment – The Director has a similar need for closure as the Powerful does, only it takes on a greater goal than a daily to-do list. They want to make a difference in the world. This could be a project completed in their lifetime or one needing completion in generations to come. They also have a daily to-do list, but it's more complex than most, maybe involving monthly, weekly, daily, even hourly spreadsheets.

Consideration of their feelings – There is a paradox in this personality blend. Even though Directors are tough as nails on the outside, their feelings can be easily bruised by the people closest to them. They will give clues to their pain, but most likely the people around them will only notice the emotional distance that is now the new normal in the relationship. If others ask what is wrong, they will calmly say they are fine, which is not true. Heart-felt apologies (without excuses) go a long way to meeting this emotional need.

Private Space – Directors are part extravert and part introvert, which gives them the ability to enjoy large numbers of people, but they have to find a place and time to decompress and reset their minds and agendas. This space doesn't need to be large, but it must be private as it will be almost sacred to the Director's personality type. To show respect and love toward the Director, do not rearrange or invade this space.

Understanding Emotional needs

Proper - Blue

Alone time - Propers are very happy being by themselves for long periods of time. This private personal time is where they can let their hair down, and be themselves. It's like removing the corset of propriety from around their middle, so they can breathe freely. Much of their creative thinking happens during this time; artwork, music, writing, analytical thinking, which all helps recharge their emotional energy. The moment another person enters this space, the corset is back on, so knock before entering this private time.

Silence - being able to analyze is one of the Propers' greatest strengths. In order to turn their analytical radar off and recharge, the outside world needs to be silenced, in order for the inside world (mind, will, emotion) can be quieted down and equilibrium regained. The easiest way to accomplish this is to separate from noise. A Proper may look like a hermit because of this.

Understanding - Propers have a systematic way to do almost everything, but they have a hard time verbally communicating this process. They need others to understand there are steps and procedures they need to work through before they can relay the information properly.

Sensitivity to their feelings - Propers want you to *feel* what they feel. They do not think they should have to *tell* you about it. If you see them in crisis, they do not want you to fix their problems for them, just be sympathetic to the cause of their pain. Trying to make them *happy* will only increase their internal stress. They will act happy to get others to stop trying to make them happy. Just support them when they're down.

Diplomat – Teal

Private down time – Any personality type that shares the Blue corner needs privacy and for the Diplomat, this privacy is reserved for their personal down time. They have the ability to compartmentalize their thoughts, so while at work or at a gathering, they are thinking about what is required of them at that time, so when they have personal down time they do not want to share it with anyone. They have already given all the energy they have. It may look like they are hiding from people, but they aren't, they are just recharging their emotional batteries.

Compassion for their feelings – As a blend personality type, the Diplomat shares the need for comfort with the Green corner and the need for understanding with the Blue corner, which combines easily for this emotional need for compassion.

Lack of interruptions – Focus is a strength for the Diplomat, making it harder for them to switch gears. It's like their thoughts run on a cog system – first they need to open the lid, remove the cog that is running, put it in the correct storage spot, find the new cog and place it on the wheel and close the lid again. Only then are they ready to give you the audience you are seeking. They do not excel at multi-tasking. Give them the grace and time to make the adjustments needed to be fully present in the conversation or activity.

Rest – Diplomats do not have any extraverted personality traits, so rest rules this category. Fear and worry are the main energy drain for the Diplomat. They do not want to offend anyone by saying the wrong thing or commit a social faux pas, so their worry radar is almost always on in public.

Understanding Emotional needs

Peaceful -Green

Feelings of worth - Peacefuls are like a being verb, not much motion, but very important to the story. Their strengths are harder to measure, like being kind or being agreeable; their ability to *be* needs to be honored just as much as others ability to *do*. Peacefuls can see both sides of an issue. However, by not rocking the boat, their strengths and opinions get overlooked and underappreciated. Asking for their opinion or yielding the floor to them during conversations is a great way to meet this emotional need. It lets them know they are valued.

Rest = Sleep – Peacefuls are not blessed with abundant energy, so down time is a must. Guilt-free naps are in order here. Their schedules require resting spots.

Peace - minimal conflict - Peacefuls feel the conflict physically in their bodies: belly aches, migraine headaches, irritable bowel syndrome and the like. Overly opinionated people or stressful situations can send them into hiding. Even rowdy fun can be too much for them. The British WWII saying fits here, "Stay Calm and Carry On."

Comfort – In making the environment peaceful, Peacefuls try to make everyone comfortable, because this brings them comfort knowing everyone is cared for. Pushing through the pain is not a Peaceful's strong point. This may be the reason behind their limited taste palette, extra weight gain, and their reluctance to take the bull by the horns, so-to-speak.

Supporter- Yellow Green

Connection – friendship – Supporters are lovingly known as everyone's best friend. They give support, compassion, care and unconditional acceptance to their friends and family. In return they are loved, even to the point of being cherished. This one-on-one connection recharges their emotional batteries. The word *nice* is usually associated with their name.

To be noticed – It is easy to overlook a Supporter, as they are not attention seeking divas, but Supporters are usually standing close by ready and willing to lend a hand. They do not demand to be the leader, nor do they like to do things alone. They enjoy being part of the action even if it is someone else's idea.

Stress-free environment – Supporters share the Peaceful's need for a calm environment and many times suffer the same physical reaction to stressful situations; headaches, stomach problems, etc. However, they are not willing to obtain peace at all costs; a bit of drama is perfectly fine as long as it doesn't become a lifestyle. For the most part, Supporters love having a good time as long as it doesn't get out of control.

Relaxation – As a blend personality type, the Supporter needs a quieter, less hectic pace to their lifestyle like the Peaceful personality type, but they also like to have fun like the Playful personality type, but not as frantic. They may not need to nap as often as the Peaceful, but they also can't go-go-go like the Playful.

Emotional Awareness

Playful Sanguine

The Salesman
Deepest desire: have FUN!

I would appreciate:
Your attention
A hug once in a while
Your approval

You can do this by:
Letting me lighten the mood with humor
Listen to my stories & give me a hug
Accept me as I am – quit trying to shape me up

And please …
Don't constantly criticize me

Powerful Choleric

The Director
Deepest desire: get the job done

I would appreciate:
A vote in the matter
Recognition of my achievements
Your loyalty & cooperation

You can do this by:
Letting me ask my "why" questions
Giving me credit for my hard work
Lead, follow or get out of the way!!!

And please …
Don't mess-up my plans

Peaceful Phlegmatic

The Diplomat
Deepest desire: everyone get along

I would appreciate:
Your respect for who I am
Encouragement when I'm overwhelmed
Keeping the drama to a minimum

You can do this by:
Recognizing my insights as valuable
Not rushing me
Don't use me as an emotional dumping ground

And please …
Don't talk down to me

Proper Melancholic

The Editor
Deepest desire: have things done properly

I would appreciate:
Your understanding when I'm feeling down
Be sensitive to my feelings
Some space and privacy

You can do this by:
Understanding my point of view
Quiet recognition of my skills and abilities
Do not use my things without asking first

And please …
Don't question my judgment

Understanding Personality Stress Factors

Playful Sanguine

Stress Factors:
Completing and organizing paperwork on time
Being too tightly restrained

When under stress:
Goes Super Nova – Adds more activities to an already too busy schedule
Excessive Talking – Has a compulsive need to fill dead air with words

To help meet emotional needs:
Tell them at least one good quality they have on a regular basis – weekly if possible.

Give them the first 5 minutes of the day to tell their story, after that, they need to get to work.
(For this to be effective, you must listen.)

When stressed out, you tell yourself:
"What?!" Hey, what's not to love here?"

Powerful Choleric

Stress Factors:
Struggle under incompetent leadership
Lack of accomplishment

When under stress:
Becomes overly crabby – has a bite to their voice, even when not angry
Takes over/usurps authority – feels a need to set things straight, with or without authority to do so

To help meet emotional needs:
Tell them you appreciate all the hard work they do even if there is no benefit to you.

Help put in place systems that get the job done. A sense of accomplishment will defuse the urge to take over or incite mutiny.

When stressed out, you tell yourself:
"This is stupid! I don't need to put up with this!"

Peaceful Phlegmatic

Stress Factors:
When there is backbiting, and bickering.
Asking them to do too many things at once is completely over whelming

When under stress:
Peace at all costs –They will compromise moral standards and lie, telling you what they think you want to hear, in order to keep the peace.
Takes procrastination to an art form – Becoming paralyzed by the fear of having to work overly hard.

To help meet emotional needs:
Make time to listen to what they have to say. Do not ignore them or treat them as if they are stupid because they are quiet.

Break larger projects down into smaller parts, so the job isn't so overwhelming. Having to make too many decisions all at once causes emotional paralysis.

When stressed out, you tell yourself:
"I need a nap"

Proper Melancholic

Stress Factors:
Fighting feelings of discouragement, when working within an incompetent system.
Not enough time to do it properly

When under stress:
Becomes silently irritated and withdrawn – communicating displeasure by giving the "cold shoulder." Retreats into their own thoughts.
Becomes vindictive, holds a grudge – Justifies "holding hostage," information and support.

To help meet emotional needs:
Respect their personal space. DO NOT touch or borrow their things without asking their permission.

Listen with full and undivided attention to the research and information they have compiled.
(Give them the time they need to do this research.)

When stressed out, you tell yourself:
"Watch your back...I will get even"

The Same, but for Different Reasons

Playful Sanguine

Talk:
Anytime - Anywhere - to Anyone. Playfuls are storytellers and salesmen. The happier they are, the louder they get.

Leader:
Playfuls lead like a Pied Piper. People gravitate towards them because there is action going on around them which looks exciting.

Lazy:
Playfuls don't like anything that's not fun. When life becomes WORK they either disappear altogether or find some way to make the work feel like play.

Fear:
Fear happens after the event takes place. Playfuls are known for their "leap before you look " approach to life.

Depression:
Playfuls are naturally optimistic and can handle plenty of stress, but under extreme restrictions or condemnation their ability to bounce back diminishes and depression sets in.

Play:
Play is what a Playful does best. It will include laughter, people, movement and FUN – no matter where or when!

Powerful Choleric

Talk:
Instructional and to the point. Powerfuls are people oriented and need others to help get the job done.

Leader:
Powerfuls are the "natural born leaders." They always have a plan and a purpose. They assume everyone will want to do it.

Lazy:
Powerfuls may look lazy when actually they are really just boycotting the activity – "If I can't win, I'm not playing the game."

Fear:
Powerfuls have deep emotions, but are fearful or uncomfortable showing the "softer" emotions. The only emotion openly permitted is anger, giving them a false sense of control.

Depression:
When life is not under their control: sickness, money problems, wayward family members, etc., and they can't fix the problems, Powerfuls tend to emotionally implode. After the anger, comes depression.

Play:
Work is play for a Powerful. They play hard and play to win! They do not tolerate wimpy team members.

Peaceful Phlegmatic

Talk:
Peacefuls are normally quiet and prefer to talk one on one. They tend to say what you want to hear – words that comfort you.

Leader:
When placed in leadership a Peaceful's style is more of a shepherd; personal on-on-one, caring and full of grace. People follow them, because they like and respect them.

Lazy:
Peacefuls are low energy people, so they may look lazy. They aren't driven to fix life's imperfections or problems, so it takes more to spur them into action.

Fearful:
Peacefuls are timid and can be easily bullied into things they don't want to do. They are not fast thinkers and get caught in crossfire, so it's safer to stay away from conflict of any kind, turning into homebodies.

Depression:
Depression can set in when there is too much stress and trauma. When a Peaceful is depressed they sleep more than usual, and become reactively crabby when normally they are light-hearted.

Play:
Peacefuls for the most part play quietly: Cards, reading, table games, video games and can become surprisingly very competitive, even though they are naturally easy going.

Proper Melancholic

Talk:
Only when Propers feel safe, will they open up. Sometimes it will be like an emotional purge -- many issues, topics and words all at once and then it's back to silence or quiet propriety.

Leader:
A Proper's leadership style is cautious and premeditated. Titles are important, have meaning and are to be respected. Proper decorum is the standard.

Lazy:
Propers are not usually lazy, but when they stop producing it may be they are emotionally paralyzed or overwhelmed.

Fearful:
Propers second guess their decisions because of what others may think. When fear gets out of control and they imagine scenarios that "could" happen, and then respond as if they have happened.

Depression:
Even though they may behave "down" or "blue," this is not the same as being depressed. Death thoughts are natural for Propers, but be aware and seek help if these thoughts become suicidal.

Play:
Propers are deeply, but privately passionate. Here is where their passion has freedom of movement: in music, drama, sports, the arts or even pursuing forbidden fruit.

Tips for Living in Personality Strengths

Now that we have identified our strength and struggles, what do we do next?

Practice being aware!
Start by developing your strengths and minimize your struggles.

Playful Sanguine	Powerful Choleric
Get it together	*Let it go*
Start:	**Start:**
Listen more – talk less	Realize others may be right
Keep track of your commitments	Apologize when you hurt others, even when you didn't mean to hurt them
Say only half of what you are thinking	Schedule time off for rest and enjoyment
Reward yourself **after** your work is done	Ask nicely – instead demanding
Tone down the volume of your voice	Use "please" and "thank you"
Be on time – this shows respect	
Stop:	**Stop:**
Interrupting others	Assuming you are right about everything
Over committing to too many projects	Fixing other people – they don't like it
Making excuses for your behavior	Blasting others with your opinion

Peaceful Phlegmatic	Proper Melancholic
Buck it up	*Lighten up*
Start:	**Start:**
Find your real interests and do them	Look for the positives in life
Trust your own abilities	Give of your time to others
Resist doing everything the easy way	Speak up **before** things go wrong
Communicate your feelings and ideas	Develop your artistic side
Stand up for what is right, instead of giving in to peer pressure	Lighten up – life is not that bad
	Take control of your thought life
Stop:	**Stop:**
Yielding to avoid controversy	Punishing yourself for being imperfect
Procrastinating about everything	Taking everything personally
Stalling, so others do your work	Making others guess at what you are thinking

Communication Styles

Each personality type has its own way of communicating thoughts, desires and information. By understanding another personality's communication style or language, we can have fewer misunderstandings, that lead to hurt feelings and broken relationships and more pro-active progress. On these two pages there are visible clues and tips for both the communicator and the listener.

Visible Clues

Playful Sanguine

The Noise Maker

Communicates with personal information
Expressive body language
Talks to anyone, about anything, at anytime
Laughs easily
Loud voice, even when talking softly
Physically touchy - feely
Is a dramatic storyteller
Becomes long winded
Uses funny expressions

Powerful Choleric

The Plan Maker

Wants to know the bottom line first
Doesn't like chit-chat, "Get to the point"
Moves on when they have grasped the concept
Talk is full of intensity
Gives quick commands or "orders"
Doesn't like drama
Emphasizes point by pounding
They can be a "bony finger in your face"
Likes to complain about things they feel are stupid

Peaceful Phlegmatic

The Peace Maker

Speaks with a soft voice
Displays dry humor – brilliant "one liners"
Is hesitant to jump into conversations
Looks for kind things to say about others
Has a relaxed body stance
Likes to listen more than talk
Avoids conflict
Tells you what you want to hear
Is easily overwhelmed when too many
    people are talking at once

Proper Melancholic

The Rule Maker

Is private with personal information
Thinks through thoughts before speaking
Needs to feel safe before opening up
Body language is close to the body
Shares information on a "need to know"
    bases
Likes the proper way of communicating –
    Robert's Rules of Order
Communicates well through the arts
Withholds opinions or information until
    asked to share it

Communication Tips

Playful Sanguine

If you are Playful Sanguine practice:

Tone down volume
Practice listening -- don't interrupt
Limit wordiness and conversation
Practice conveying only what is needed
Practice remembering other people's names
If interrupted, only continue a story if asked
Share the stage
Include everyone in conversation
Say only half of what you think

If you are speaking to a Playful Sanguine:

Tell people stories
Give colorful details
Give acceptance
Don't tune out – pay attention
Give them approval for who they are

Powerful Choleric

If you are Powerful Choleric practice:

Request (not demand) action from others
Practice saying "please" and "thank-you"
Be careful of your tone of voice
Broaden areas of interest
Stay put (do not pace or leave while talking)
Focus interest/attention on person not project
Actively listen -- don't cut others off
Read to the end of the letter
Hold back on giving your opinion

If you are speaking to a Powerful Choleric:

Give bottom line first
Keep communication short and to the point
Give appreciation for their hard work
Give supporting details only if asked or critical
Accept curtness, but not rudeness

Peaceful Phlegmatic

If you are Peaceful Phlegmatic practice:

Speak up with volume and information
Express your opinions
Share ideas
Practice making choices
Show enthusiasm with body language
Listen with interest, without judging
Speak more quickly; ask for help
Think through presentations in advance
Speak the truth in love

If you are speaking to a Peaceful Phlegmatic:

Show respect -- don't talk down to them
Give a few choices, not orders
Freely give praise
Learn to say, "I appreciate you, because _____."
Give focused attention when they are talking
Wait to speak until they are completely finished

Proper Melancholic

If you are Proper Melancholic practice:

Adjust expectations/perfection rarely happens
Receive compliments graciously
Celebrate even the smallest of improvements
Build others up even when you don't feel good
    about yourself
Practice saying out loud two positive thoughts each day
Practice making positive observations
Be careful of being overly critical while analyzing
Remember; different is not wrong
Don't overwhelm others with details

If you are speaking to a Proper Melancholic:

Ask them if it's a good time to talk; don't barge in
Don't interrupt while they are talking
Respect time/space/silence/schedules
Give factual orderly details, not chit chat
Be sensitive to their needs, laugh and cry with them
Think through what you will say ahead of time

History of Personality Typing

Greek Influence

As with all scientific research, and theory building, knowledge comes in stages. Personality typology has followed the same developmental path; one thought building upon another. Its origins started in the early Greek medical world, linking illness, cause and personality behavior all together. It took thousands of years of observation, theory building and research for our modern personality typing systems to come into being. The first theories of earth elements and humors which were thought to control illness and cures may not have been entirely accurate, but the observations of human behavior have stood the test of time. The following is a brief overview of the major stages of personality typing.

Four Elements
Water, Earth, Air, Fire

It was **Empedocles** (490 - 430 B.C.E.) who first established the idea of four ultimate elements which make up all the structures in the world - fire, air, water, and earth. In his elements theory, nothing new comes or can come into being; the only change that occurs is a change in the alignment of element with element. Empedocles believed the only way elements moved or changed, were through the power of Love and Strife. Love was the force which caused different forms of matter to become attracted to each other, and Strife accounts for their separation or being pushed apart. Empedocles was the first medical scholar to link human behavior as a measurement for the alignment of the four elements which are influenced by love and strife.

Four Humors
**Sanguine, Melancholic
Choleric, Phlegmatic**

Hippocrates (460 - 370 B.C.E.) affectionately known as the *Father of Modern Medicine*, was more than a medical doctor and teacher, he was the inspiration for a new approach to the practice of medicine. He was an astute observer of his patients, carefully recording their symptoms, the way their illnesses developed, and the reaction to treatment, coming to the new realization that diseases came from natural causes – the body's humors being out of balance. The Greeks felt the body humors or fluids, along with the four elements controlled personality behavior. His observations of human behavior were for the most part correct, only we now know temperament, or personality is linked to our DNA and environment, not body fluids.

**Four
Temperaments**
Warm, Cold, Moist, Dry

Galen (131 - 201 A.C.E.) was the man who formalized the idea of the *temperaments*. He appropriated the best of Greek thought - Hippocratic medicine, Plato, and Aristotle to form new medical theories. Building on the Greek foundation of humors and elements, Galen added his own observations to explain human behavior. He added the qualities, **warm, cold, moist or dry**, in which a combination of two, warm and moist, warm and dry, cold and dry or cold and moist, dominated. These four combinations were eventually named after the Greek humors they represented, **Sanguine** (warm-moist), **Choleric** (warm-dry), **Melancholic** (cold-dry) and **Phlegmatic** (cold-moist). While the term *temperament* came to refer mainly to psychological dispositions, Galen used it to refer to bodily dispositions, which determined a person's susceptibility to particular diseases as well as behavioral and emotional inclinations. Even though some of Galen's theories were proven to be incorrect, modern medicine/science still upholds his message as sound advice: observation and investigation were required for thorough medical research.

In stitching together the correct parts of past theories, time has proven Empedocles' theory that love and strife attract and repulse to be true: we are drawn to love and avoid strife if at all possible. Hippocrates' observation of human behavior as accurate: Sanguine types are more "hot blooded," while Choleric types tend to be more impatient, the Melancholic nature is more susceptible to emotional ups and downs and the Phlegmatic type moves at a bit slower pace than the rest. Galen added his observation of warm or cold, moist or dry. Today we may refer to it as introvert or extravert, friendly or suspicious. If we are willing to appropriate the insightful observations of the past and apply that knowledge to new research, we will be one step closer to understanding *What Makes You Tick*.

History of Personality Typing

Modern Influence

Sigmund Freud

So, how did modern medicine/psychology make the jump from Greek theories to today's personality typing systems? Modern personality systems are not the product of one school of thought or one person's research, but a combination of science, philosophy, and theology. **Sigmund Freud** (1856 – 1939) opened the door to the unseen world of the mind. He introduced the idea of the subconscious, where the invisible power of the Id, Ego and Superego control our behavior. If you agree or disagree with Freud's theories, the fact remains his theories opened up dialog in the study of human behavior.

Carl Jung (1875 - 1961) a student of Freud's, disagreed with some of these theories and decided to follow a different line of research, one that viewed humankind as more than just flesh and bone, one with a spirit as well. He took the idea of the subconscious to a deeper level, that of *the collective unconscious* where the commonalities of a group, species or society are stored subconsciously in each individual. Through this research he formalized the idea of archetypes (*The Shadow, The Anima, The Animus, The Self*), different parts of each person's psyche. Jung also disagreed with the *abula - rasa* theory of human psychological development, where humans are believed to be born blank slates, so to speak, and the imprinting of our environment dictates who we become.

Carl Jung

Katharine Briggs Isabel Briggs-Myers

Katharine Cook Briggs (1875 - 1968) encountered Jung's ideas in 1923 by reading his book *Psychological Types, The Psychology of Individuation*. This resonated so deeply with her that she made it her life goal to make this information available to the world, not just academic societies. Along with her daughter **Isabel Myers** (1897-1980), they began two decades of "type watching," or observing, and after adding their own observations to those of Jung, Isabel Myers began creating a paper-and-pencil questionnaire to assess personality types in order to help people understand each other better and avoid conflict. The Myers-Briggs Type Instrument (MBTI®) was developed over the next three decades.

At around the same time Katharine Briggs was introduced to Jungian thought, **Dr. William Moulton Marston** (1893–1947), a Harvard scholar, authored a book in 1928, *The Emotions of Normal People*. In this book, Marston identified the building blocks of behavioral responses as Dominance, Influence, Submission (now Steadiness) and Caution (now Compliance) which became the foundation for the DISC assessment system. Later, Dr. John Geier purchased the copyright to Marston's work and in 1958 created the initial DISC assessment profile, revising it in the 1980s with the help of his long-time associate Dorothy Downey.

Dr. Wm Marston

Almost all modern personality systems assign a color and an adjective to each type or type blend to help identify the basic nature of that personality trait. As more research findings become available, such as the Genome Project, more discoveries reveal knowledge about human nature, helping answer the question, how much of our personality is hard wired and how much is learned?

Personality Principles ™ assessment system is based on a combination of Greek observations and terminologies; Sanguine, Choleric, Melancholic and Phlegmatic and modern research and observations: Carl Jung's idea of commonalities, Erik Erikson's viewpoint on environmental influences in personality development, Alfred Adler and Kevin Lehmann's research on birth order, Marston and Florence Littauer's perspective on emotional needs, and the new information coming out in the Big 5 personality research, and of course, concurrent observation.

Other popular contributors to modern personality profiling systems:
Florence Littauer (1927-) *Personality Plus*, Tim LaHaye (1926-) *Spirit Controlled Temperaments*, David Keirsey (1921-) *Please Understand Me*, Don Riso (1946 -) & Russ Hudson (1948 -) *Personality Types* (RHETI), Henry Alexander Murray (May 13, 1893 – June 23, 1988) *Perspectives on Personality*, Oscar Ichazo (1931-) the **Traditional Enneagram**, D. W. Fiske (1949 -) *Big Five Dimensions of Personality* and expanded upon by Warren Norman (1967-), G. M. Smith (1967-), Lewis Goldberg (1981-), and R. R. McCrae & P. T. Costa Jr. (1987-) *NEO Personality Inventory*. Robert A. Rohm, Ph.D. (1954 -) *Personality Insights*.

Questions & Answers

Q

"I feel putting a person's personality in a category is limiting, why would I want to do this?"

A

It may feel like pigeonholing someone's personality or putting them in a box, but it's just the opposite. It's freeing to understand who we really are. When we understand our personality strengths and struggles, we can direct our energy toward maturing the behaviors that are struggles for us, and focus more on developing our natural strengths. We can celebrate being who we are, instead of trying to be someone we are not.

Q

How can I be sure the profile results are accurate?

A

Doing a personality assessment is not like taking a test, there are no right or wrong answers. If you answered the questions as honestly as you know how, then your score should reflect it. If you are still not comfortable with the result of your assessment, have a friend or family member answer the questions for you and see if their results match yours. Remember, self discovery is a journey. It may take a while – be patient and look for the clues.

Q

What can I do if I don't like my personality type?

A

Acceptance is the first step in coming to terms with who you are. It would be a good idea to examine the strengths of your personality type and focus on making those qualities the traits you are known for having. Also, by identifying your struggles, you know what areas of your life could use a bit of discipline.

Note: It is equally hard for each personality type to overcome their own set of struggles. It's better to give a bit of grace rather than condemnation when you see someone living in a personality struggle. Remember, maturity is hard work.

Q

Is there one personality type that is better to have than others?

A

No. It's beneficial to remember that one personality type is not better than another. Each personality type has its shortcomings and its strengths. It is usually the person who is living in their shortcomings or struggles that irritates others the most – no matter what their personality category.

Questions & Answers

Q *Does a person's personality change over time?*

A Your character does, but not your basic personality type. Maturity plays a huge part in your personality behavior. As you do the adult profile, think of how you behaved as a child, a teen, a young adult and an adult, make a mental note of the things that have changed - home life, career, marriage, parenthood; all of these life stages impact how we behave. Now note what personality traits have stayed the same throughout your life. You will notice behaviors that are consistent, like being talkative or the need for privacy. Even though you have learned to either quiet down if you are a talker, or open up if you are overly private, the tendency is still there. By working to live in your personality strengths and minimize your personality struggles, you can change your character, but your basic personality type still desires the same emotional needs.

Q *What is meant by the term "Blend Personality?"*

A Very few people are only one personality type. Most people are a combination of two or even three personality types all blended together. Your scores should reflect these blends. Normally the highest score is your primary personality type, with your next highest score being your secondary personality type and so on. Don't be alarmed if you have a category with a score of zero, this is normal. This shows the intensity of the other personality types in your blend pattern.

Q *What type of schooling is required to be a Personality Trainer?*

A All "certified" personality consultants or as we like to refer to ourselves, "Personologists," have attended training courses, either in person or online and have fulfilled the requirements needed to become certified. Many personality consultants have a traditional college degree in Psychology and/or are a Certified Live Coach.

Visit www.personalityprinciples.com about becoming a Certified Personality Consultant (Personologist).

About the Authors

Both Kathryn and Cassandra were separately introduced to the idea of personality differences through books written by Florence Littauer: *Personality Plus* and *Your Personality Tree*. The information presented about each personality's emotional needs became a lifeline in managing difficult relationships and situations. The principles they learned during those times became more than a coping strategy for the moment, it became a way of life, transforming their relationships with their spouses, children, co-workers and friendships.

Kathryn and Cassandra's paths first crossed while attending a speaker-training seminar (CLASServices) and it took no time at all for a new camaraderie to bloom. In 2007, Kathryn launched *Personality Principles LLC™*, adding new research and a fresh approach to the personality information that has proven to be accurate through testing and time. Since then, both women have shared this practical information at seminars, online and in-person, corporate workshops, and trade shows. As part of the *Personality Principles LLC™* curriculum, they have hosted *Advanced Personality Training Seminars* for those wanting to use this information in their businesses and careers.

We have come to realize that of all the self-help information on the market, understanding personality differences is the most powerful tool we've found in minimizing the stress and misunderstandings of everyday relationships as well as helping to create an individualized plan for a better life. It is our desire to offer an easy-to-understand personality based system to lay-people and professionals alike in order to empower happier, healthier relationships.

Kathryn Robbins is a Certified Life Coach, Personality Trainer, speaker and author. She makes her home in St. Louis, Missouri with her husband Steve and their three dogs. Only the youngest of their five sons lives at home, the rest are married and make their homes in Missouri, New Jersey, and London, England. Her children's personality profile, *The You Zoo,* is dedicated to her granddaughter.

Cassandra R. Cooper is a Certified Personality Trainer, a Virtual Assistant with special certification as an Author's Assistant and Editor of the Christmas Organizing series. She lives on her family's farm in West Tennessee with her husband John. They have two grown daughters and four grandchildren.

"If you want a thing done well, get a couple of old broads to do it." — **Bette Davis**

Personality Principles Products

Online Resources:
Online Short Profile – FREE – login from the website's home page www.personalityprinciples.com.
What Makes You Tick Online Profile – tabulates and stores your results. The Online Profile is available as a onetime use, or on a monthly subscription, great for counselors and coaches.

Hard Copy Short Profiles – excellent for workshops
Can be completed in 10 minutes

Children's Profile
With parenting tips
(Available in major bookstores and online)

Courses:

**Bringing Out Your Potential -
10 Week Course** covers all the basics of personality traits: visible clues, strengths & struggles, emotional needs, understanding the Learned Personality, relationship issues, communication styles and more.
The course is versatile enough to be taught in professional or personal settings.
The 40 page course contains:

- 19 charts
- 4 assignments
- props list
- 6 posters
- 1 hour private training

Personality Training:

Certified Basic Personality Training

- 24+ hours of dynamic teaching
- 135 page Comprehensive Notebook
- A downloadable recording of your classes
- Live - Answer/Question time on each call
- Over 35 re-printable handouts
      (worth the price of admission!)
- 2 hours of personal coaching
- Certified Personality Discount pricing on
      materials
- Able to stay in the comfort of your own home
- Monthly Newsletter
- On-going support and encouragement
      (Priceless!)
- Access to the Advanced Personality Training.

Visit the website for pricing and more information - **PersonalityPrinciples.com**

Resources

Books

Personality Plus, Revised and Expanded edition
    Florence Littauer, Revell (1992), ISBN-13: 978-0800754457
Wired That Way
    Marita Littauer and Florence Littauer, Regal (2006), ISBN-13: 978-0830738403
The Birth Order Book, 2 Rev Upd edition
    Kevin Leman, Revell (2009), ISBN-13: 978-0800734060
Men Are From Mars – Women Are From Venus
    John Gray, Harper Paperbacks (2004), ISBN-13: 978-0060574215
Stage II Recovery; Life Beyond Addiction
    Earnie Larsen, Harper One (1987), ISBN-13: 978-0062548085
Early Greek Philosophy:
    Burnet, John, AMA Publication (2012), ASIN: B006Z9UCPS
The Psyche in Antiquity: Early Greek Philosophy: Studies in Jungian Psychology By Jungian Analysts, Book 1
    Edinger, Edward F., Deborah A. Wesley, Inner City Books (1999) ISBN 0-9191-2386-4
The Dream of Reason: A History of Western Philosophy from the Greeks to the Renaissance.
    Gottlieb, Anthony, W. W. Norton & Company (2010), ASIN: B0045Y23P2
The Foundations of Personality
    Myerson, Abraham, Biblio Life (2008), ISBN 0-5543-5715-1
Explorations in Personality
    Henry A. Murray, Oxford University Press, USA; 70th anniversary edition (2007), ISBN 0-1953-0506-X
The Handy Philosophy Answer Book
    Naomi Zack, PhD, Visible Ink Press (2010), ISBN 1-5785-9226-7

Internet Resources

enneagraminstitute.com/history.asp
enneaweb.com/enneagramhistory.html
discassessment.org/history-of-disc-assessment
discprofile.com/what-is-disc/history.htm
capt.org/mbti-assessment/isabel-myers.htm
myersbriggs.org/my-mbti-personality-type/mbti-basics/isabel-briggs-myers.asp
mbtitoday.org/about-the-mbti-indicator/a-mini-history-of-the-myers-briggs-type-indicator
earnie.com/books.asp
leadingfromyourstrengths.com/pull/index.html
psychoid.net/personality-psychology-study-of-psychology.html
internal.psychology.illinois.edu/~bwrobrts/Goldberg,%201993.pdf
iep.utm.edu/galen
iep.utm.edu/hippocra
ptypes.com/temperaments.html
geierlearning.com/author.html
finestquotes.com/select_quote-category-Personality-page-0.htm#ixzz1uCc1RJmi

Pictures

petegoldlust.com
istockphoto.com
dreamstime.com
publicdomainpictures.net
123rf.com

Quotes

thefreedictionary.com
brainyquote.com

Made in the USA
San Bernardino, CA
11 October 2015